Architecture
& Programming
of
the Intel x86 Family,

40th Anniversary edition

Patrick H. Stakem

(c) 2017

Expanded, Updated, and Revised

Number 20 in the Computer Architecture Series.

Table of Contents

3

Introduction

This book is an update to an earlier book on x86 computer architecture, hardware and software. The x86 describes not only a line of microprocessor chips dating back to 1978, but also an instruction set architecture (ISA) that the chips implement. The chip families are built by Intel and other manufacturers, and execute the same instructions, but in different ways. The results are the same, arithmetically and logically, but may differ in their timing.

Why the focus on the Intel x86? It was the basis of the IBM personal computer (PC) family and its spin-offs. It has transitioned from a 16 to a 32 to a 64-bit architecture, keeping compatibility for 40 years. It's an de-facto industry standard that has withstood the test of time.

The purpose of this book is to provide the basic background information for an understanding of the 80x86 family. It will stress the pervasiveness of this pc-based technology in everyday things and events. The original book was a spin-off of a course in Computer Architecture/System Integration, taught by the author in the graduate Engineering Science Program at Loyola College (now, Loyola University in Maryland).

A pc is a computer I have on my desk, and a mainframe is a computer I can't lift. A server spends most of its time providing services (data, internet) to other computers.

How do we get a computer to do what we want? A big stick is sometimes a help. The early computers in the late 1940's and early 1950's were wired by plugboards for the sequence of instructions, and the numeric data was set in by switches. The program was run, results were obtained, and changes made to the configuration for new tasks. Faulty vacuum tubes were identified and replaced. This was a rather time consuming process.

The author's first computer experience was on a room-filling Bendix G-20 mainframe. It was a 32-bit machine, using the Algol language. His first assembly language experience was on an IBM S/360 mainframe, specifically the Model 67 variant, with virtual memory. He went on to program the Univac 1108 series mainframe (a 1's complement machine), the DEC PDP-8, 9, 10, and 11, the Bendix G-15, the Athena Missile Guidance Computer by Sperry Rand, designed by Seymour Cray, and many more. The idea of a personal computer was, at the time, ludicrous.

Introduction to the Second Edition

Since the first edition of this book was published, quite a few advances have been made in the X86 area. The author has moved on to the ARM architecture for embedded systems. But, there was a need to correct some typos and formatting issues, to clarify some material, and to add some pictures. There is not much new material included, but the concepts and discussions remain valid. A glossary was added.

Introduction to the Current (40th anniversary) edition

This new effort was triggered by the introduction of a new chip for the 40th anniversary of the x86 architecture. Who would have thought the architecture would remain commercially viable at the time? This gives us a unique opportunity to see how Moore's law has held up over time, and to compare and contrast the 40-year old part with the current one, to understand where we are coming from, and heading to.

I removed a lot of the basic material from the original including discussions of the number systems, data structures, I/O methods, etc. These are generic, and can be found in many Introduction to Computer Science texts.

I have added details on the newer chips, did a compare and contrast with the original 8086, and included some material on AMD's rival x86-architecture chips.

Author

The author has a BSEE in Electrical Engineering from Carnegie-Mellon University, and Masters Degrees in Applied Physics and Computer Science from the Johns Hopkins University. During a career as a NASA support contractor from 1971 to 2013, he worked at all of the NASA Centers. He served as a mentor for the NASA/GSFC Summer Robotics Engineering Boot Camp at GSFC for 2 years. He teaches Embedded Systems for the Johns Hopkins University, Engineering for Professionals Program, and has done several summer Cubesat Programs at the undergraduate and graduate level. He is involved in global colloborative projects, mostly relating to space.

Limitations of the technology

The microelectronic used in pc's has some basic limitations imposed by the laws of physics. The speed of light (186,000 miles per second, or 300,000 kilometers per second) sets an upper limit to how fast we can communicate. No information flows faster than the speed of light. System complexity and testability sets limits to the implementation of systems. Quantum effects become important, as we use smaller and smaller features.

The basis of microelectronic technology is clean sand, silicon being the semiconductor material of choice. It is cheap and plentiful. We use etched 2-dimensional structures to define the devices. Most are made by photochemical means. We don't have practical (i.e., cheap) 3-dimensional structures that are manufacture-able (yet).

Microprocessor chips generate heat when switching, or changing state. This is a tiny amount, but there are hundreds of millions of transistor switches, so the chip-level heat generation get gewt beyond 100 watts. This represents a cooling problem, requiring fans. More importantly, silicon is a poor heat conductor, and small scale features inside the chip may get close to melting temperature due to restricted heat conductance. This has limited chip switching speeds. The use of different substrates can help alleviate the thermal problem. For example, diamond is an excellent thermal conductor, although somewhat pricey.

And then there's Moore's Law. In 1965, Gordon Moore of Intel observed that the number of transistors per area on integrated circuits doubled every 18 months. It continues to do so. For how long? Moore's law is more of an observation, not a law. It comments on our ability, not our limits. It is an exponential growth law, and there are multiple laws, one for computing, one for memory, one for communication. Exponential growth is not sustainable in the long run. We'll see a little later on how it's doing, when we compare the original 8086 to the 40th anniversary chip, the Core i7-8086k.

Hardware Elements of a Computer

This section will discuss the hardware components of the Intel x86 family. Starting in 1978, Intel introduced the 16-bit 8086 as a follow-on to the 8-bit 8080 processor. The family continues today, 40 years later. It retains the same basic architecture as the earliest chips, and so constitutes a valid family of devices.

X86 Processor family

The 80x86 processor family began with the 8086 and 8088 models in 1978 and 1979. Stephen O. Morse lead the work at Intel. These chips were followed by the 80286 in 1982. Each of these had an associated floating point coprocessor, the 8087 and 80287.

The architecture was extended from 16 bits to 32 with the introduction of the 80386 in 1985, and its associated coprocessor, the 80387. The '386 and its associated coprocessor, were available in 16-bit external bus versions, the SX series. The 80486 in 1989 combined the coprocessor and the main processor on the same chip. In addition, many other companies (such as AMD, NEC, IDT, Texas Instruments, IBM, OKI, Fujitsu, Siemens, and others) also produced these chips and variations under license. The commonality was the ISA-86. The floating point coprocessor for the 80386 was the 80387. The 80486, and subsequent chips, incorporated the floating point unit on the same chip as the integer processor.

The 8088 was the 8-bit external bus version of the 8086. Each memory word took two accesses. This was to save cost on the memory architecture. The 8088 was chosen by IBM to be the basis of their PC architecture. Embedded control versions of the architecture were introduced as the 80188 and 80186. These included some additional devices on the same chip, to reduce chip count in a system, while maintaining compatibility with the ISA-86.

8

These devices were designed to ease the transition from 8-bit to 16-bit, by allowing legacy code to still run. The 80286 chip introduced Protected Mode, an arrangement to extend the addressing capability beyond 1 megabyte to 16 megabytes. The 80386sx was also introduced with an "8088-like" interface. The 80386sx and 387sx used a 16 bit memory interface. For a while, the 80286 was actually faster at executing instructions than the 80386 (at the same clock rate), but this advantage was rapidly overtaken by increasing clock rates.

The 80386 featured a 32-bit real address, and 32-bit registers. It had a 46-bit virtual address, with an on-chip memory management unit (MMU) to translate virtual to real addresses. There were now 6 instead of 4 segment registers, optional paging support in the MMU, hardware support for multitasking, and some new instructions. The 80386 supported memory management by segmentation in the new Protected mode. The '386 I/O supported 16- and 32-bit I/O using adjacent I/O space byte addresses. The 32-bit flags register was a superset of the 16-bit one, with the lower 16 bits being identical, and new flags in the upper part.

Operating systems such as OS/2, UNIX, Linux, bsd, and Windows take advantage of Protected Mode's advanced features. For example, multiple copies of DOS can run under UNIX, sharing system resources transparently. The 640k memory barrier of DOS is artificial.

There were three new control registers in the 386, six debug registers for breakpoint addresses. There were additional registers to support segmentation. The 80386 had three modes of operation. Real mode made it a big strong 8086 with 32 new instructions, 2 new segment registers, and the debug registers.. Virtual-86 mode added MMU functions for paging and a multitasking environment. Protected mode was the big change. The earliest 80386's could use the 80287 math coprocessor, but that changed when the 80387 became available.

There were also third-party floating point processor chips that were compatible.

The floating point coprocessor in the Intel architecture executes from the same instruction stream as the main processor. For operand fetch, the coprocessor uses a memory cycle steal, something like a DMA operation as far as the main processor is concerned. The coprocessor has its own set of internal registers, organized as a stack. Registers are 80 bits wide.

The Intel numeric coprocessors also do operations on extended precision integer (64-bit) and floating point format. They are faster than the main processor in these operations, and, in addition, operate in parallel with it. For example, a 64x64 bit multiply would takes 2100 microseconds on the 8086, but only 30 microseconds on the 8087 coprocessor, a speed up of a factor of seventy.

The Intel processors and associated coprocessors form a tightly coupled pair. The main processor does all the instruction fetching. In addition, it is responsible for transferring data to the coprocessor's registers. Execution of coprocessor instructions proceeds in parallel with those of general instructions. The coprocessor recognizes its own instructions, and executes them. Coprocessor instructions start with a hex F. The main processor ignores coprocessor instructions. Between the main cpu and the coprocessor, there is a busy/wait handshake mechanism for coordination. There is a control word and a status word in internal registers in the floating point unit. The floating point unit also maintains its own instruction pointer and an operand pointer. The floating point unit can generate exceptions including invalid operation, attempted division by zero, normalization, overflow, underflow, and inexact result.

The instruction set includes load and store; the basic add, subtract, multiply, and divide; compare; square root; and certain pre-calculated constants in floating point format such as zero, one, pi, $\log_2(10)$, and others.

The 80486 added the MMU and the floating point functionality onboard the same chip, with a small 8 kilobyte on-chip data and instruction cache. More operations became single cycle, and string operations were faster. A barrel shifter provided faster shifts. The internal data buses were wider, for faster data transfer. The '486 introduced the Byte Swap instruction to reverse the endianess of data items. This allowed easier access to IBM mainframe and Apple-Motorola data. In addition, if the 80486 tried to access data that was misaligned, an interrupt was generated. This condition is transparent to the running program, but slows it down considerably.

Other x86 implementations that used emulation or translation of X86 instruction to internal RISC (reduced instruction set computer) instructions included NexGen Nx586, the PowerPC 625, the IMS 6250, the Toshiba R4x00 Tigershark, which translated x86 to MIPS, and others. By the introduction of the Pentium-II and Pentium-III, Intel was also translating x86 to an internal optimized RISC instruction set.

At this point in the technology curve, not only could large amounts of cache memory be included with the cpu chip, but multiple cpu's could be included in one package, a technique referred to as multicore. The Pentium is, essentially a pair of '386's plus a '387. Intel's patented technique of hyperthreading refers to a simultaneous multithreading implementation in Pentium 4 and subsequent processors. Multiple threads of execution are supported. The hardware plus the operating system software operate with two virtual processors per physical cpu core. This approach is transparent to the software. It is not quite as fast as having two physical processors, but is certainly faster than one.

The x86 architecture was extended to 64 bits, the IA-64. This includes not only 64-bit addresses and data, but significant levels of instruction parallelism, using speculative execution, branch prediction, a register stack, and other optimization techniques. It remains binary compatible with IA-32.

11

Instruction level parallelism provides an avenue to higher performance, at the cost of complexity. We include additional hardware, with the overhead of managing and coordinating this hardware. One technique is instruction re-ordering at run time, in hardware. This means the hardware examines the instruction flow to recognize and exploit opportunities for parallelism. We can also try to predict branches. Your first guess would be that you would be right ½ the time. For something like a loop structure, you could be right most of the time, if you guessed that the branch was taken. In the control speculation approach, we move loads and their dependencies above branches. In data speculation, we can move loads above possible conflicting memory references. With control flow prediction, we guess, and take the consequences. Unwinding the results of a wrong guess may not incur a large penalty. Another approach is to execute down two branch paths simultaneously until the branch is resolved. The correct path is continued, and the incorrect path is discarded.

Virtual-86 mode was introduced in the 80386 as an 8086 emulation mode. The 80386 can implement multiple 8086 environments running "simultaneously" in protected environments. These are virtual machines. There are some minor differences in how memory above 1 megabyte is treated.
.

Page level protection was implemented on the 80386 and subsequent processors. This involves a user/supervisor bit, and supervisor write protection. Paging uses smaller, fixed-size memory blocks. Segmentation uses larger, variable size blocks. Page mode is enabled with a single bit. It can be used with segmentation, as an additional layer of protection, with additional overhead. Pages in the x86 are 4096 bytes, at an address divisible by 1000_h. The page directory and tables are used to control the pages. CR3, the control register, has the page frame address or the page directory in the high order 20 bits. The page directory can hold 1 million entries. Each entry is a pointer to a page table. The page table contains pointers to physical memory.

Around the time of the Pentium introduction, other companies were producing chips that used the x86 architecture, mostly under license from Intel. These included Cyrix, Nexgen, Via Technologies, and Transmeta. AMD holds a license from Intel for the x86 as well.

Cyrix merged with National Semiconductor in 1997. It held no license from Intel, but rather had reverse-engineered the Intel product. This lead to some legal battles that were fought to a stalemate. Finally, the companies cross-licensed each other's products.

Transmeta, acquired by Novafora, which has since gone out of business. Has licensed its tech to Intel.

Nexgen was purchased by AMD in 1996. It's chip translated x86 instructions on the fly to its internal RISC architecture.

Via Technologies manufactures x86 and motherboard chipsets. It is based in Taiwan.

Atom

The Intel Atom cpu is a 32-bit x86 architecture optimized for low power. It was introduced in 2008, and is available in multicore and hyper-threaded editions, with speeds beyond 2 GHz. There are generally three models – N for low power, Z for mobile devices, and D for low-end desktop and D for low end laptop and desktop. It translates x86 instructions into internal RISC instructions on the fly, and can execute two integer instructions per clock. Because the parts are IA-32 and IA-64 compatible, there is a large amount of available legacy software available. System-on-a-chip devices based on the Atom were available in 2012, targeting the IoT market. The SoC devices were built in a partnership with Google, and were meant to run the Android operating system for phones and tablets. The Atom was roughly comparable to an ARM

Cortex-A8 in performance, but has a factor of 4 more power draw. The Atom features in-order instruction execution, and has branch prediction. It has a relatively slow divide. The SSE unit is faster in doing floating point calculations than the built-in floating point unit (x87). The Atom supports Intel's real and protected modes, as well as hyperthreading, where each physical processor core can support 2 logical cores. This technique increases the utilization of the execution unit, which can be both good and bad. They also have a Turbo Boost feature, where they can be overclocked for brief periods, limited by heat generation. This involves both clock rate and voltage. There is also hardware support for virtualization, and support for security with trusted execution. The x86 architecture scales, as we have seen from the original 8086 in 1978, to the latest Atom model. It also now supports 64 bits, as an architecture extension. The x86 processors use a version of the 8086-era 8259 Interrupt Controller. With the 8086, it was a separate chip. Now it is included with the cpu, but works the same. Interrupt vectors are kept in protected memory.

The Atom processor, E3900 series, and it's companion units, the Celeron-based N3350 and Pentium-based N4200 directly address the Internet of Things. All come in a quad-core configuration, and are implemented as a module (compact flipchip ball grid array). The N3350 operates up to 2.4 GHz. All of the models support up to 8 gigabytes of DRAM. The 4200 has a Pentium with a 2 megabyte cache, and operates up to 2.5 GHz. The Atom-based units have 2 megabytes of cache.

Atom has some features targeted to the embedded world, such as Intel's Speedstep, which is a low power sleep mode. It does support JTAG. Ubuntu released a special version of its linux for Atom-based netbooks, called Ubuntu Netbook Remix.

The E3900 model can have a dual or quad core, with an associated image processor (the IMPU4), dma; SATA connections, 6 USB-3 and 2 USB-2, 3 SPI, 1-SDIO, and support for an SD card. The high performance graphics unit can have up to 18 execution units. There are dual audio DSP's, and it can interface up to four MIPI-CSI cameras. There are four PCI-express ports.

The Atom does in-order execution, 2 instructions per clock. It does support the CPUID instruction, introduced with the 80486. This instruction returns identification data on the cpu, as well as cpu features. Software can then tell what cpu version it is running on.

The Atom has on-chip instruction trace, via JTAPG.

X-86 virtualization

X86 virtualization allows for multiple x-86 operating systems to share base x86 resources simultaneously, and is an example of hardware virtualization. This was originally done by complex software. Hardware support included in newer generations of cpu chips vastly simplified the process.

In Intel's defined Protected mode, the operating system kernel runs at a high privilege (ring 0) and applications at a low privilege level such as ring 3. One approach is to run the hypervisor at ring 0 privilege, and the operating system at a lower level. Certain operating system instructions require certain ring levels to be able to execute, however. Binary translation can be used to replace these with other instructions that will execute at a lower level. The process is called trap and emulate, but this involves overhead.

Hardware support to virtualization, provided by both Intel and AMD, involves both the privileged instructions, and MMU support. These were implemented in different ways.

Intel-VT

Intel's initial hardware virtualization support, called "Vanderpool" was released on Pentium 4 models in 2005. I/O virtualization can be enabled in the BIOS.

AMD-V

AMD's approach to virtualization support was initially called AMD Secure Virtual Machine, and was available in 2006 on the Athlon-64 series of chips. A second generation virtualization approach, simply called AMD virtualization, involved an AMD-developed technique called Rapid Virtualization Indexing, using nested page tables. The presence of virtualization support can be determined by accessing the CPU flag.

Intel Core series

The Intel Core series addresses the high end workstation and server market, making the Pentium the entry level chip. This series includes the i3, i5, i7, i9 and the Y-series. There are enough variations on these chips to require a book of their own. The 40th anniversary part is a Core i7. Intel considers it an 8th generation part.

The original Core product was a 32-bit dual-core X86, based on the Pentium-M. The Core series began to implement the 64-bit architecture with the Core-2, and extended into the four-cpu Core Quad. The i3 introduced a new micro-architecture, the Nahalem, in 2008. The Core-i7 used one of seven new microarchitectures. The new generation used the Ivy Bridge microarchitecture. A microarchitecture is how the instruction set execution is handled internally to the chip. It implements features such as pipelining, branch prediction, superscalar operation, out of order execution, and register renaming.

Core i7-8086k

Let's do a quick compare of the specs for the original 8086, and the Core I7-8086k.

Gen	chip	cores	year	arch	clock	transistors
1	8086	1	1978	X86	5 mHz	29,000
8	Core i7-8086k	6	2018	X86	5 gHz	10^9

The 8086 supported just one thread of execution, but in the Core-i7, each core supports two threads of execution, for a total of 12. It has 12 megabytes of cache per core. It supports dual memory channels, and requires a motherboard with a 1151 pin socket. It requires a premium heatsink/fan to get rid of its 95 dissipated watts.

The actual module is 4.6 x 4 x 2.75 inches. It uses DDR4 SDRAM.

AMD Ryzen

The AMD Ryzen addresses the high end desktop, is in direct competitor to the Intel Core series, and uses the same instruction set. The highest end chip at the moment is the Threadripper. It features 16 cores, and processes 32 threads of execution. It uses a 3.4 GHz clock, that can be boosted to 4 GHz. It uses a 4094 pin socket. It came out in August of 2017.

Moore's Law

Gordon Moore was a co-founder of Intel. He speculated that the number of transistors in integrated circuits would double every two years. This is somewhat because the next generation's fabrication facilities are built with the current generation of chips. We get better as we get better. Is there a limit, a wall? Of course. We're not there yet. Let's look at the 8086 and the new kit, the Core i3-8086k.

The 8086 had 29,000 transistors. The Core i7 has several billion. So, the number of transistors in the chip has increased by a factor of 100,000 in 40 years. Interestingly, the transistor size has decreased by a factor of 20,000. Smaller transistors are faster.

Let me wave my hands and say an increase of 128,000, since I want to do this in binary. So, in forty years, we have an increase factor of 128,000 or 2^{17}. That's 17 doublings in 40 years, or approximately a doubling every other year. Close enough for scientific work. :^}

Instruction Set Architecture (ISA) of the 80x86 Family

Program (definition):
A magic spell cast over a computer allowing it to translate input statements into error messages

The ISA of the 80x86 family is defined by Intel Corporation. Besides Intel, numerous other manufacturers make or have made 80x86 family members and derivatives. Specialized embedded versions of the 80x86 ISA evolved. The instruction set has been emulated in software on competing processors, such as the IBM/Motorola/Apple PowerPC. The instruction set was emulated in hardware in chips such as the IMS 3250, or the PowerPC 615.

The original ISA was a 16-bit architecture, extended to 32-bits with the Pentium series of processors. The next generation of chips are a 64-bit architecture, the extension to ISA-64, which maintains compatibility with ISA-32.

Programmers model of the x86

The Programmer's view of the x86 Instruction Set Architecture (ISA) includes:
The memory model, the registers (data), and the instructions (operations on data).

The Intel 8086 was a 16-bit processor, circa 1978. It was designed as a follow-on to the earlier successful 8-bit 8080 processor. There were big advantages in going to a 16-bit word, and the associated 8087 co-processor provided floating point capability. Software comparability was not maintained.

The 8086 provided fourteen 16-bit registers. Four of these were general purpose, and there were four pointer/index, four segment, a flags register, and the program counter. With 16 address bits, the processor could addresses 1 megabyte of memory. There were 135 basic instructions, including multiply and divide, and many variations. The chip provided support for the BCD data format, and had a separate I/O space with 65,000 input and 65,000 output ports. The I/O ports were 8-bits in size.

Status flags are automatically set by ALU operations, and can be read by the program. These allow for the implementation of data dependent branches, like "branch on zero." The status flags include:

- Carry flag, CF, set on high order bit carry or borrow.
- Parity flag PF, set if even.
- Aux. Carry - key to BCD operations, set on carry or borrow from lower 4 bits to upper 4 bits.
- Zero flag – ZF, set if results were zero.

19

- Trap flag - if set, interrupt occurs after each instruction.
- Interrupt enable (programmer settable) - if not set, cpu ignores interrupts
- Direction flag - set by instruction, controls direction of string moves, high to low, or low to big.
- Overflow flag - set if signed result cannot be represented

The Intel x86 instruction set

This section will discuss the storage elements on the cpu chip (the registers), the logical and arithmetic operations on data, and the ways to change the flow of control in the program. The principals are the same for any digital computer, but the implementation varies.

The registers

First, we need to introduce the registers, which are temporary working memory on the cpu chip itself. They hold data items temporarily, and can serve as inputs to, and the output from the arithmetic logic unit. Some registers are involved in addressing memory. The cpu has other registers that are not visible to the programmer.

The default register size is 16 bits. The general purpose registers are named AX, BX, CX, and DX. Each 16-bit register is actually two adjacent 8-bit registers.

AX = AH, AL
BX = BH, BL
CX = CH, CL
DX = DH, DL

The 16-bit registers were extended to 32 bits. These general purpose registers are called EAX, EBX, ECX, EDX. (extended AX, etc.). The AX register is the lower 16 bits of the 32-bit EAX register, just as the AL register is the lower 8 bits of the 16 bit AX.

The 16-bit pointer/index registers are: SP, BP, SI, DI. These are the stack pointer, the base pointer, the source index, and the destination index registers. Pointer/index registers hold addresses.

The extended 32-bit pointer index registers are ESP, EBP, ESI, EDI. Extended stack pointer, etc. These registers were also extended into 64-bit versions.

Interrupt architecture

The 80x86 architecture has a single interrupt request line, and a corresponding acknowledge line. Interrupts can be prioritized by external hardware (the interrupt priority controller) up to 256 different ones. The PC architecture has 8, the AT architecture has 15. Intel's interrupt controller is the 8259 chip, priority interrupt controller. It manages 8 interrupts and is cascade-able, using 1 input to chain to another device. Interrupt with the highest priority are recognized first.

External interrupt sequence of events:

- Processor is happily executing instructions, when...
- A nasty external device signals for attention on the interrupt request line. If the interrupts are enabled,...
- The processor completes the current instruction, and signals acknowledgment on ACK line.
- The interrupting device puts an 8-bit code on the lower 8 lines of the databus.
- The processor reads this code, multiplies it by 4, and jumps to that location.

- Hopefully, this gets us to an interrupt service routine.

Interrupt vector table (IVT)

In real mode, the IVT is in the lower 1024 locations of RAM. It is a table of addresses. Each entry is 4 bytes, the new CS and the new IP register contents. Who sets this up? It is the operating system's responsibility. There must be a valid entry in each location, otherwise an interrupt might go off into never-never land.

Interrupt by software

INT xx is the interrupt instruction, which causes a synchronous interrupt. It is repeatable and cannot be masked. It can generate any possible interrupt, including those reserved to hardware conditions (divide by 0, for example). Execution of the instruction kicks off a sequence just like an external interrupt would. This provides a convenient inter-process communication mechanism. It is used by the BIOS (interrupts 00 to 1F) and the DOS (interrupts 20 to 3F).

Interrupts from external sources

External interrupts are asynchronous, by definition. The processor never knows when they will happen. The timing is controlled by the external I/O device.

Variable length instructions in the architecture make it hard to predict exact interrupt response times. They can be bounded, however. Remember that the lengthy string instructions are interrupt-able.
The priority of external interrupts is generally higher than that of the executing program. The Operating system software sets and manages priorities.

Exceptions are interrupts caused by internal condition, usually the result of instruction execution. They are synchronous to the execution of instructions.. Examples are:

Fault - reported before the instruction is executed.
Trap - reported during execution of the instruction
Abort - severe error. No restart possible.

We can choose to ignore interrupts by software, all except the non-maskable interrupt.

If we use the instruction, CLI - clear interrupt flag, the processor will not recognize maskable interrupts. We really want to have the interrupts locked out for as short a time as possible, because the interrupts are a necessary part of system I/O. We can also use the instruction STI - set interrupt flag, for the processor to continue to recognize and respond to interrupts. Interrupt handling is transparent to the running program, and it leaves the processor in the same state as before the interrupt occurs.

An Interrupt service routine (ISR) is a small subroutine that responds to the request for service by the external device. It is terminated by an IRET instruction, the return from interrupt. This gets the returns address off the stack, and returns to the point where the cpu was executing, before the interrupt occurred. A lot of ISR's are written in assembly for speed. Writing hardware-specific ISR's is something of an art form. It requires in-depth knowledge of the hardware on both sides of the interface.

The INTO instruction generates software interrupt 4, if the Overflow flag (OF) is set.

For simultaneous interrupts, there are defined rules of priority. These depend on the specific processor, and can be found in the manufacturer's data sheet..

Processor-reserved interrupts

Some of the 256 possible interrupts in the x86 architecture are reserved by the chip manufacturer for specific purposes. In the PC board architecture, more interrupts are reserved for specific I/O functions. Intel, the chip manufacturer, reserved the interrupts 00 thru 1Fx, but not all are defined.

The processor-defined interrupts:

00 = divide error
01 = single step
02 = NMI (non-maskable interrupt)
06 = invalid opcode
08 = double fault
0D = general protection fault
0E = page fault

An exception occurs after the execution of an instruction. The resulting flag is cleared, the single-step handler is executed in normal mode. It resets the flag before exit. The 80386 and subsequent have built-in debugging features, relying on interrupts.

NMI

The non-maskable interrupt is the highest priority external interrupt; it cannot be masked by software. This feature came about because of an oversight in earlier processor design. It the hardware allowed the software to mask all of the interrupts, there is the possibility of getting into a state that you could not get out of, except for turning off the power. Since that time, all processors have an interrupt that cannot be ignored by the software.

Invalid opcode interrupt

On the 80286 and subsequent, this signals an attempt to execute a bit pattern not defined by Intel as a valid opcode. Before this, the case could happen, with unpredictable results. 8086/8088 chips made by different manufacturers did different things when these undefined bit patterns were executed. It was an exciting time for programmers. In the Intel 80286, the $D4_{16}$ opcode set the AL register to the value of the carry. Undocumented opcodes were generally not supported in the assembler with mnemonics, but could be defined directly in hex. With the invalid opcode trap, undocumented op codes became obsolete. This is interrupt 06_{16} in the Intel scheme of things.

Double Fault interrupt

This is an exception during the handling of an exception. This is very bad. It means we had two protection violations during the execution of a single instruction. The processor goes to shutdown, and we need to RESET. This is an obscure case that shouldn't happen if the operating system is on its toes. (Do operating systems have toes?)

Advanced double fault interrupt

It just gets better on the 80386 and subsequent processors. They became smarter (more clever) in unraveling multiple faults. There are now two categories: benign faults and contributory faults. Some of these double faults are recoverable. This is the operating system's responsibility.

General protection fault interrupt

This is mostly associated with protected mode. It signals an attempt to write into a read-only segment. This can be caused by somehow treating the stack as read-only, or treating the data as execute-only. This is an operating system issue.

Page fault interrupt

On the 80386 and later, this signals an error detected during address translation where a page is not present in memory. This happens a lot in virtual memory management, and is handled by the operating system.

Addressing modes on the 8086

Segment registers in the x86 architecture select a 64k byte block (addressed by 16 bits) out of a 1 megabyte address space (provided by 20 address lines), in real mode.

Segments start on 16 byte boundaries (because segments are multiplied by 16, or shifted left by 4 bits).These are called paragraphs.

There are 64k different segment starting addresses; in each, the 4 low order address bits are zero. Segments may overlap, but it complicates things.

Effective Address Calculation

The x86 does not have a flat directly addressed space like most processors. It is a complicated scheme. We'll discuss the processor's calculations of the effective address.

The Bus Interface Unit (BIU) Segment Base Registers

The processor can address 1,048,576 bytes of memory and requires 20 address lines in real mode. The internal registers of the processor are 16 bits wide and can only generate 64k different addresses. The designers of the x86 architecture decided to have each 64k segment start on a paragraph address. A paragraph address is always a multiple of 16.

Notice that the 4 lower bits of the paragraph address are always 0; therefore, the paragraph address can be expressed as a sixteen bit binary number with the 4 lower bits implied. The paragraph address of the 64k segment is stored in a segment base register located in the BIU.

The 8086/88 had four segment base registers called the code segment (CS), data segment (DS), extra segment (ES), and the stack segment (SS). When an instruction references memory, the paragraph address (shifted left by 4 bits) of the proper segment is added to 16-bit address provided by the instruction. The result is the 20 bit address in the physical memory. The 16-bit address, provided by the instruction, is called the OFFSET within the segment or the effective address.

As an example, suppose an instruction is referencing location 1234h in the data segment. Further, let us assume the paragraph register for the DS segment contains 2001h.The physical address, within memory, is calculated as follows:

paragraph register shifted left 4 bits = 20010h
plus offset of data within segment =   1234h
                                       ----
physical address in memory=   21244h

The virtual address is expressed as XXXX:YYYY, where XXXX is the contents of the segment base register and YYYY is the offset within the segment. The virtual address of the above is: 2001:1234 SEG:OFF.

$$SEG * 16 + OFF = ADD$$

Example: 2001:1234=>21244 hex

20010   ;shifted left by 4 bits, lsb's = 0

```
 +1234
------------
 21234
```

Memory Segments

There are four segment registers in the original x86 architecture, with default assumptions as to which segments they are pointing to.

The CS or code segment register points to the area where instructions to be executed are stored. The IP or instruction pointer contains the offset address within the code segment of the instruction to be executed next.

The DS or data segment points to the area where data references will be made. The DS is also used to specify the source for string manipulation instructions. The offset address is provided by the instruction.

The SS or stack segment points to the area where the stack will be placed. The offset within that area is provided by the Stack Pointer.

The ES or extra segment may be used for data, or destination operands of string manipulation operations. In the 386 and subsequent, there are also the two additional FS and GS segment registers.

Code addressing modes

Code addressing is much simpler. The CS register points to the code segment, and the Instruction Pointer (or, Program Counter) provided by the hardware provides the offset. Only a direct address is used. This will be the address of the next instruction to be executed, as automatically calculated by the hardware. Since the instructions are variable length, we need the calculation.

Data Addressing Modes

Data addressing is more complicated. An instruction usually specifies a source and a destination. These can be registers or memory or the stack. In different modes of addressing the address is known (or, resolved) at different times. Some of the modes are complicated, and little used. They can simplify the addressing of complex data structures, such as multiple-dimensioned arrays.

Format: Instruction Destination, Source

where destination = memory or register
        source = memory or register or immediate

Details of Addressing modes:

Register to register addressing is straightforward; not all combinations are valid. You need to check the instruction syntax.

Immediate to register or memory has a value calculated at assembly time, and included as part of the instruction. No string constants greater than 2 characters are allowed.

In direct addressing, the contents of the symbolic memory address are source and destination; and the value is calculated at load time.

In indirect addressing, the register contents are considered as an address; the value is calculated at run time. The indirect modes use the BX, BP, SI, or DI registers. Memory operands default to the data segment, except when BP used as a base register, when the stack segment is assumed.

In Base + displacement mode, a fixed displacement is added to the address. This could be an offset in a table, for example.

In Base + index + displacement mode, the contents of a register + the contents of an index register plus a fixed displacement form the address.

The Segment Override Specification is used to access data in a different segment than the default one.

example:

MOV AX , ES : [BX]

A word within the extra segment at an offset equal to the contents of BX will be moved into register AX. Recall that the Extra segment is a Data-type segment.

Program Flow

JUMPS

Jumps implement changes in the flow of a program. They can be unconditional or conditional. The unconditional jump is always taken; it is the GOTO. The conditional Jump depends on the result of a previous calculation in the program, as contained in the flags register.

LOOPS

Loops are control structures that are executed for a number of iterations times, or are executed until a calculated condition is met.

TEST BITS & JUMP

In terms of jumps, we must consider the concept of distance to the referenced label. This is the number of memory bytes (the difference in addresses) of the referring and the referenced items. From the current instruction, labels may be in one of three distance categories:

Short   -128 to + 127 bytes away

Near   -32768 to 32,767 bytes away, but in the same segment

Far   in a different segment

A short reference only needs 1 byte of address specifier, and a near reference needs 2 bytes. A far reference needs 4 bytes. Two hold the offset, and two hold a new segment address.

A J U M P does a transfer unconditionally to a specified address:

syntax:

        J M P operand

where operand := register or address

The register contents or address value is used with CS to form a new effective address, which is then used to update the IP register.

Examples:

        J M P Label1

Label1:   jump target

This instruction generates 3 bytes of code, as Label1 is a forward reference, and the assembler must assume a near jump (within the same segment, but greater than 127 bytes away). If you know that the target address is within 128 bytes, you can force a short jump:

        J M P   S H O R T Label1

This has the effect of generating a 2 byte (instead of 3 byte) instruction that executes slightly faster. This will also generate a warning message. If the target is more than 127 bytes away, an error message will be generated. For backward (previously defined) references, this procedure is not required.

In the case of far jumps case, the target address is in another segment, and a 5 byte instruction is generated:

J M P FAR PTR Label1

The PTR (pointer) operator forces the operand Label1 to have the type FAR. A total of 4 bytes is required to specify the new segment (2 bytes) and the offset (2 bytes).

Conditional jumps involve a two-step process: test the condition, jump if true; continue if false.

Syntax:

CMP   operand 1, operand 2
J XX   address

where:

operand 1 := register or memory
operand 2 := register, memory, or immediate
XX   := condition
address   := short

To use near or far conditional jumps, either reverse the sense of the test and use a near or far conditional jump, or use the conditional jump to jump to a near or far unconditional jump instruction.

LOOPS are used for iteration control.

Syntax:

LOOP x Address

means:

C X = CX - 1

if CX = 0, fall thru, else jump

There are also forms that allow us to terminate loop early. The loop involves short jumps only, so there is a maximum size.

The Loop instruction is placed at the end of the loop; it jumps back to the beginning. This means there is at least one iteration through the loop. We need to initialize the repeat count before entering the loop.

X86 Boot sequence

How does the processor get started? Upon power on, a special hardware circuit generates a RESET signal to the processor. RESET is a special type of interrupt. The RESET signal takes the processor to a known state. All of the registers will contain known values, defined by the manufacturer. Specifically, the program counter contains a specific address for program start. For the Intel x86 architecture, this is at the top of memory. Thus, we need a Jump instruction at the top of memory, to a bootloader routine. This can be implemented by having some non-volatile memory at the top of the address space.

The 8086 reset

When you hit the red button, what does this do? Well, it causes a special interrupt to the processor.

Several registers are set to particular values:

```
IP  = 0000h    ; instruction pointer
CS = FFFFh    ; Code Segment register
DS = ES = SS = 0000h        ; data, extra, and stack
```
segment registers.

After reset on the 8086, the processor accesses an address 16 bytes below the top of memory, fetches the instruction from there, and executes it.

What is 16 bytes below the top of memory? Well, that's the key question. Part of the Operating System, specifically the BIOS, is responsible for putting a proper value there. Since the address is only 16 bytes below the top of memory, we can't put much of a program there, but we can put a Jump instruction to anywhere else in memory.

So, what's there? Again, the Operating System is responsible for putting a program there, that does whatever we want to do after a RESET. Do a clean-up, restart a program, etc.

If there isn't something valid in those locations, the process still continues, but the results may be less than desirable.

The BIOS ROM

This section of read-only memory is provided by the board manufacturer, and is a bootstrap program to initialize the processor, and load in an operating system.

At the high end of memory, we need a persistent copy of the code that will be executed in the case of a reset. This was accomplished by putting the program in ROM, and putting it there in the address space. Since the 8086 could only address one megabyte of memory, this simply put an upper limit to the useable memory.

And, at that time, system didn't have (couldn't afford) a megabyte of memory anyway. With later processors being able to address larger memory spaces, the BIOS ROM stuck at the first megabyte of memory was a pain. It remains that way.

At the low end of memory 0000h, we need some RAM, some memory to read and write. Advanced processor's reset is similar to that of the 8086, in that it initializes in real mode. This because the BIOS is not compatible with Protected mode.

The contents of this memory has come to be called the BIOS, the basic input output system. It does hardware initialization, some testing (POST), and has a boot loader. The boot loader is a piece of code just smart enough to load the rest of the operating system from files on a secondary storage device, such as a disk or flash memory. The process is called, pulling yourself up by your bootstraps. The default loader gets some code from a known location on the storage device, loads it into memory, and jumps to the code. This rudimentary loader can then load the operating systems (or, perhaps, one of several operating systems) from the storage medium.

Power On Self Test, or POST, executes a rudimentary series of tests of the system components. This is incredibly difficult, conceptually, because the computer hardware tests itself. Assumptions must be made about minimal functionality. The POST part of the BIOS function is probably the most interesting part.

CPUid instruction

An interesting exercise to see if we understand the hardware, is to write a program to determining the processor hardware we are running on. Actually, with the introduction of the CPUid instruction with the Pentium processor in 1993, it is very easy. We just ask the processor what it is. Before the Pentium, we had to make use of processor idiosyncrasies of the processors, executed in the right order, to figure this out. It was also possible to identify which company made the processor. Made for a good homework assignment.

Today, code reads the processor type to see what series of optimizations should be applied. Optimizations for one implementation may be exactly the wrong thing to do for other implementations.

LoadALL instruction

The LOADALL instruction (OF, 05) was an undocumented opcode introduced with the 80286. There is a completely different LOADALL (0F 07) for the 80386, and after that, the instruction was discontinued. In the early processors, not all bit codes were valid instructions, and the ones that were not valid instructions were not necessarily ignored. Some non-valid bit patterns actually did something useful. However, these bit patterns would not necessarily work with X86 processors from other manufacturers. Now, un-implemented instruction codes default to an interrupt.

The LOADALL is a deliberate instruction, kept out of the general instruction list. Its function was to load all of the CPU internal registers at once. This allowed cpu states not generally allowed in the X86 programming model. It required 195 machine cycles to complete, and used a 102 byte area in memory starting at address 0800_{16} to hold the entire set of processor state information. It was a backdoor method of getting out of protected mode without a reset on the 80286. The 80386 Loadall was undocumented and not supported by Intel. The hex code was OF 07. It loaded a 204 byte area pointed to by the ES:EDI register pair into all of the internal registers. That covered the entire internal execution state information.

LOADALL was used by utilities to gain access to additional memory without leaving REAL mode. This was used by the utility HIMEM.SYS. It would also allow a 16-bit protected mode. This was used in Digital Researche's Concurrent DOS 286 operating system. LOADALL could also enter a real mode with paging support on 386's.

With full protected mode operating systems, the LOADALL instruction was not needed.

Self-Modifying code in x86

First, understand, self-modifying code is evil. You should never do it. It is all Von Neumann's fault, because he erased the line between the code and the data.

Actually, the assembler writes "data" into the code area. What we are talking about here is a running program modifying itself as it runs. Sometimes that seems like a clever way around a tough problem, but it is extremely difficult to debug if something goes wrong.

Code can modify itself during an initialization phase based on a menu of input parameters. This eliminates a lot of conditionals, and reducing program size. We can also have a program that modifies itself as it runs, overwriting instructions with new ones. Essentially, we have dynamic instruction creation.

Some higher order languages allow for code to be modified, while others (Python, JavaScript) allow programs to create new code at run time, which is then executed.

Self-modifying code has been used to conceal such features as copy protection, or viruses or malware. Some operating systems control the write-ability of the code segment.

In systems with cache, writing to memory might actually only be writing to the cache, which has a finite lifetime.

Trivia Question: Which instruction in the x86 architecture assembles to 00 00 00 00 00 00 00 ?

Answer: ADD [BX+SI], AL

Protected mode

Protected Mode was introduced on the 80286. There were some issues.

The DOS operating system was not compatible with Protected Mode. One can enter Protected Mode from DOS, but not necessarily get back. Protected Mode was introduced on the 80286 to extend the addressing capabilities of the x86 architecture beyond one megabyte. The 8086 native mode is called REAL mode.

Protected mode on the 80286 is of some academic interest only, because there is no way of returning to real mode, except by a hardware reset. It is referred to by some as virtual mode. The concept was that setup would be done in real mode after reset, and the system would transition to Protected mode for subsequent operations.

Operating systems such as OS/2, UNIX, linux, bsd, and Windows take advantage of Protected Mode's advanced features. For example, multiple copies of DOS can run under UNIX, sharing system resources transparently. The 640k memory barrier is artificial.

The 80286 and 80386 enter real mode at reset. This mode is comparable with 8086. By software, you can command an entry to protected mode. On the 80286, it isn't easy to get back to real mode via software. On the 80386 and subsequent processors, you can.

In protected mode, you have all the features of real mode, plus:

- Virtual addressing

- More memory addressable (16 Mb vs. 1 Mb on the 80286)

- Protection mechanisms for operating system software

Protected Mode offers advanced features that can be used by operating systems to support multitasking.

Virtual Addressing

The physical address space is what you have to work with. The virtual address space is what you pretend to have to work with. The processor does the dynamic mapping between virtual and physical address. This memory management technique is called address translation, and requires additional overhead on each memory access.

On 80286, physical address is 2^{24} = 16 Megabytes, and the virtual address is 2^{30} = 1 gigabyte.

With virtual memory, you can write applications that assume you have 1 gigabyte available, and rely on the operating system to swap the correct virtual memory pages into and out of the existing physical memory. This, of course, takes time.

Memory beyond 640k without protected mode is possible, but it involved a lot of overhead. First, we need to look at memory classifications.

In conventional memory, there are 10 segments of 64 k each - "more than any programmer could ever need." The 640k barrier is at $A0000_h$, with the display mapped memory being placed there.

Extended memory is memory beyond 1 megabyte on the 80286 and subsequent. It needs a memory manager program, such as himem.sys.

Expanded memory uses gaps between 640k and 1 megabyte. It maps up to 16 megabytes of memory into these gaps, using a manager, written to the LIMM specification (Lotus-Intel-Microsoft). It was used for DOS applications, not for Windows, which has its own manager program.

Virtual memory

We can use hard disk space used as memory, in the form of a swap file. Disk memory is much less expensive than semiconductor memory, but much slower as well. The virtual memory is mapped through regular memory. In additional to the penalty of the speed, there is extensive software overhead as well in the translation process. Thrashing refers to the scenario where the system is caught up in swapping memory, without getting anything else done.

The upper memory area was the 384k above 640k, in the DOS world. There is system hardware mapping in this area, for example, for the display adapters, the BIOS in the pc architecture, and BASIC in ROM in the IBM pc architecture. Unused memory gaps are called upper memory blocks (UMB).

The high memory area is the first 64k of extended memory. Through a quirk of the addressing scheme, this can be addressed in real mode.

To understand the physical address calculation process in protected mode, we should first review the Physical Address Calculation in real mode. There is a 16-bit segment specifier plus a 16-bit offset. The address is in two 16-bit parts, a segment and an offset. We shift the segment part over to the left by four bits (or, equivalently, multiply it by 16), and add the offset. We get a 20-bit result.

Physical address = segment * 16 + offset

This provides a 20-bit physical address which spans $2^{20} = 1$ megabyte of address space.

(now it gets complicated)

In protected mode, there is a 16-bit segment selector plus a 16-bit offset to yield a 32-bit virtual address. The virtual address is what the running program uses. The system converts the virtual address to a physical address (in real time) that goes out over the memory bus to the system's memory. There is more virtual memory than real memory. The bookkeeping is handled by the system, partially in hardware and partially in software.

Along with protected mode, Intel introduced the ring model of privilege, modeled on the Unix approach. There are 4 layers, where the innermost is the most trusted, and the outermost is the user program.

The base address of the segment in memory is not calculated by multiplying the segment specifier by 16, but rather by indexing a table in memory. This table, previously set up by the program or operating system, is called the descriptor table. It contains more than just the address translation information.

The Selector Table contains entries called selectors. Selectors contain three fields:

> The Requested Privilege Level (RPL),
> The Table Indicator (TI), and
> Index (I)

The RPL field does not concern address translation, but is used by the operating system to implement privilege level protection. It is a number 0-3. The intent is to prevent a less-privileged program from accessing data from a more privileged one.

The TI field specifies the table to be used by the Global Descriptor Table (TI = 0) or the Local Descriptor Table (TI = 1). These are data structures residing in memory, and set up by the operating system. Global Descriptor Tables are pointed to by the Global Descriptor Tables registers. The Descriptor Table Registers can be read and written by specific instructions; the GDTR by the instructions LGDT and SGDT, and the LDTR by LLDT and SLDT. On the 80286, there is one GDT, and each task can have its own LDT.

The Index is a pointer into the table. Descriptors are 8 bytes long. The index item is a 24-bit address for the corresponding segment (on the 80286. 32-bits on 80386 and subsequent).

The 24-bit address obtained from the selector table look-up is added to the 16 bit offset to form a 24-bit physical address. Overflows are ignored, thus addresses wrap around.

If TI = 0 (GDT) and Index = 0, this is the null selector. If it is used for address translation, it results in an exception.

The index field is 13 bits, so a descriptor table can have up to 2^{13} descriptors. Each describes a segment of 2^{16} bytes. So, each task can have a private memory space of 2^{29} bytes. A segment is 64k bytes on the 80286. On the 80386 and subsequent, with 32-bit offset addresses, the virtual address space is 2^{46} bytes.

Segment descriptors are located in the descriptor table. They consist or two parts, a base address and a limit. They contain status and control information for access. They provide a link between a task, and a segment in memory.

Memory descriptors specify a type, code or data. Code is executable, data can be read-only or read-write. These distinctions are imposed by the data structure; the memory is Von Neumann, and read-write. The Type field differs for code and data. The code segment can be accessed, can be readable or not, and is conforming or not. The data segment can be accessed, writable or not, and expands up or expands down (like a stack).

The access byte contains an indicator bit about whether the segment is physically present in memory or not.

Swapping and Mapping

The maximum amount of physical memory was 16 megabytes, so disks are used to hold other virtual pages that are mapped into and out of physical RAM by the operating system.

Further complication of protected mode includes the fact that the math coprocessors ('287, '387) also have a protected mode, and interrupt servicing in Protected Mode involves an Interrupt descriptor table, interrupt gates, and call gates.

In protected mode, calling and jumping involve an inter-segment FAR call through a call gate. The privilege level of the caller is checked against the privilege of the called program (in the gate descriptor). It the level is not good enough, a general protection fault (INT $0D_h$) is generated.

Before entering protected mode, all of the necessary data structures such as the descriptors tables, must be properly set up. This is an operating system function. Then the LMSW (load machine status word) instruction is executed, with the PE (protection enable) bit = 1. Simple. BUT.... First, the instruction queue must be flushed. This is because the instructions were fetched in real mode, but are to be executed (now) in protected mode. How do we flush the queue? Simply do a short jump to the very next location beyond the jump. Jumps force an instruction queue flush. The astute reader will notice that the short jump is fetched in real mode and executed in protected mode, but that's ok – it works.

Exiting protected mode on the 80286 required a RESET or the Loadall instruction. On the 80386 and subsequent, return to real mode simply requires resetting the PE bit by instruction.

Another concept that came along with Protected Mode was that of tasks. There can be many tasks in the system, only one running at a time. These are controlled by the operating system (itself a task) with the TSS- Task State Segment structure. This contains the task state (essentially, register contents). The processor has a task register for the currently running task that is user-visible. There are also pointers (not visible) to the TSS. The Task register is loaded and stored with the LTR/STR instructions. The TSS descriptor looks like a descriptor that we have talked about, but has an idle/busy bit. Tasks are not re-entrant under this scheme.

The Task gate descriptor is an indirect, protected way of accessing a task. It resides in the GDT. A task that does not have enough privilege to use the TSS descriptor can call another task through a gate in the LDT.

Task switching is managed by the operating system, and involves controlled calls and jumps. Interrupts are also managed.

Virtual-86 mode was introduced in the 80386 as an 8086 emulation mode. The 80386 can implement multiple 8086 environments running "simultaneously" in protected environments. These are virtual machines. There is some minor differences in how memory above 1 megabyte is treated.

Page level protection was implemented on the 80386 and subsequent processors. This involves a user/supervisor bit, and supervisor write protection. Paging uses smaller, fixed-size memory blocks. Segmentation uses larger, variable size blocks. Page mode is enabled with a single bit. It can be used with segmentation, as an additional layer of protection, with additional overhead. Pages in the x86 are 4096 bytes, at an address divisible by 1000_h. The page directory and tables are used to control the pages. CR3, the control register, has the page frame address or the page directory in the high order 20 bits. The page directory can hold 1 million entries. Each entry is a pointer to a page table. The page table contains pointers to physical memory.

MMX Extensions

The Pentium processors introduced a single-instruction multiple-data (SIMD) extension to the architecture called MMX, MultiMedia Extension, in 1997. It included eight new 64-bit registers. These registers are meant to hold eight 8-bit integers, four 16-bit integers, or two 32-bit integers, which will be operated upon in parallel.

The MMX registers are actually mapped into the floating point registers, making it tricky to do floating point and MMX operations simultaneously. The floating point registers are 80 bits wide, and the MMX registers use the lower 64 bits. The MMX extension has continued in the IA-32.

MMX supports saturation arithmetic. In this scheme, all operations are limited to a fixed range between a defined minimum and maximum. Values beyond those limits are not recognized. The mathematical properties of associativity and distributivity are not applicable in saturation arithmetic. An alternative to saturation arithmetic is where the values wrap-around, which unfortunately changes the sign in twos-complement representation. For audio processing (louder-than-loud) and video processing (blacker-than-black), saturation arithmetic works fine. It's the issue of getting an answer "close enough) in the time allowed. Saturation arithmetic plays an important role in digital signal processing techniques for video and audio processing.

In 1997, AMD released an enhanced MMX architecture called 3DNow! which added 32-bit floating point to MMX's integer operations.

In 1999, Intel went to the SSE architecture with the Pentium-III, and later the SSE2 with the Pentium 4. This refers to Streaming SSE has new 128-bit registers, and corresponding instructions. An SSE and a floating point instruction cannot be issued in the same cycle, due to resource conflicts. SSE2 brought double precision floating point support. SSE has 70 additional instructions to support operations from digital signal processing and graphics.

SSE3 added new digital signal processing features, and SSE4 added an instruction for vector dot product.

Advanced Vector Extensions (AVX) introduced a 256-bit data path, and 3-operand instructions. These are extensions to the x86 architecture. These units can operate on 256 or 512 bit data structures. AVX-2 extends integers to 256 bits, and adds bit manipulation and multiply. AVX-512 extends data and operations to 512 bits. Vector data can be loaded from non-contiguous memory locations, referred to as gather, and stored to non-contiguous locations, called scatter. Exponential and reciprocal instructions accelerate transcendental functions. They implement the fused multiply-add operation, which looks like: X = round (*a* × *b* + *c*).

Tolapi

This is an Intel system-on-a-chip, based on a Pentium M core, with included I/O and security. The current clock rates extend to 1.2 GHz. It has a 256k onchip cache, and supports DDR external ram. There is extensive I/O and interfacing support. These units support the instructions MMX, SSE, SSE2 and SSE3.

TSX-ni is an architectural extension to IA-86, the Transactional Synchronization Extensions. This supports transactional memory to simplify concurrent programming. Essentially, in transactional memory, a set of load or store instructions can be concurrent.

Intel x-86 Embedded

This section discusses the x-86 embedded architecture, built around the x86 Atom processor, with added features for the embedded environment. This takes the form of included memory and I/O, so we can have a single chip solution.

Intel Quark

The Intel Quark SE is a 32-bit x86 architecture SOC. The cpu operates at 32 MHz. It does not support floating point operations, but does have an 8-kbyte instruction cache. The sensor subsystem includes a 32-bit Argonaut DSP-RISC core which does support floating point, and a hardware-based pattern matching accelerator, with 128 "neurons." There is 384 kbytes of flash memory, and 80 kbytes of SRAM, which is shared between the processors. There are 5 timers, one of which is the watchdog. For I/O, it supports dual UART's, dual SPI, usb, 32 GPIO's, and 2 general purpose i²c's and 2 master-only i²c's in the sensor section. The are also dual i2s and 19 analog comparators (no A/D). The system has 8 dma channels. All of this is on a 10mm x 10mm package.

The Zephyr small-footprint Open Source Kernel OS runs on the Quark processor core. It is a project of the linux foundation, that Intel contributed to.

The architecture also has the XD (execute disabled) bit for security. This allows memory pages to be marked as data-only. This counters software exploits and buffer-overflow attacks.

The Intel Galileo board was based on the Quark SoC X1000, and was the first Intel board that was hardware and software compatible with the Arduino shields. It is now retired.

Intel Curie

The Intel Curie SOC Module is a 32-bit System-on-a-chip, using the Quark processor. The module can be hosted on a development board, with interfacing connectors. The module was announced in 2015.

The integrated digital signal processor based sensor hub interfaces with the included BOSCH BMI160 6-axis accelerometer/gyro. These devices are interfaced via SPI. There is also a I²C interface for an external magnetometer. JTAG is supported.

There is a pattern matching engine, that identifies motions and activities, using the 6-axis sensor. It compares these with previously stored values in memory. The device includes a low power Bluetooth module, for wireless interfacing with external devices. The module footprint is 11 x 8 mm in size, and 2 mm tall. The device comes with a bootloader in flash, that can be re-installed over JTAG.

Intel Edison

The Intel Edison is a System On Module (SOM) that is the basis for the Arduino-101 board, and the Edison Break-out board, which is a little bigger than an Arm-based Arduino. It has a dual-core, dual-thread 32-bit Atom cpu operating at 500 MHz, and a 32-bit Quark microcontroller operating at 100 MHz. The Edison is also the basis of the somewhat larger IoT Analytics board, which interfaces with aps on the Cloud for data analytics.

Wrap Up

The x86 architecture has stood the test of time, and has seen may doublings of processor performance over 40 years. Here's to 40 more! By that time, we'll all have an x86 machine implanted at birth, with enough ROM to boot us up.

Glossary of Terms and Acronyms

1's complement – a binary number representation scheme for negative values.

2's complement – another binary number representation scheme for negative values.

Accumulator – a register to hold numeric values during and after an operation.

ACM – Association for Computing Machinery; professional organization.

ALU – arithmetic logic unit.

ANSI – American National Standards Institute

API – application program interface; specification for software modules to communicate.

ASCII - American Standard Code for Information Interchange, a 7-bit code; developed for teleprinters.

ASIC – application specific integrated circuit, custom or semicustom,.

Assembly language – low level programming language specific to a particular ISA.

Async – asynchronous; using different clocks.

Babbage, Charles –early 19th century inventor of mechanical computing machinery to solve difference equations, and output typeset results; later machines would be fully programmable.

Baud – symbol rate; may or may not be the same as bit rate.

BCD – binary coded decimal. 4-bit entity used to represent 10 different decimal digits; with 6 spare states.

Big-endian – data format with the most significant bit or byte at the lowest address, or transmitted first.

Binary – using base 2 arithmetic for number representation.

BIOS – basic input output system; first software run after boot.

BIST – built-in self test.

Bit – smallest unit of digital information; two states.

Blackbox – functional device with inputs and outputs, but no detail on the internal workings.

Boolean – a data type with two values; an operation on these data types; named after George Boole, mid-19th century inventor of Boolean algebra.

Bootstrap – a startup or reset process that proceeds without external intervention.

Buffer – a temporary holding location for data.

Bug – an error in a program or device.

Bus – data channel, communication pathway for data transfer.

Byte – ordered collection of 8 bits; values from 0-255

C – programming language from Bell Labs, circa 1972.

Cache – faster and smaller intermediate memory between the processor and main memory.

Cache coherency – process to keep the contents of multiple caches consistent,

CAS – column address strobe (in DRAM refreshing)

Chip – integrated circuit component.

Clock – periodic timing signal to control and synchronize operations.

CMOS – complementary metal oxide semiconductor; a technology using both positive and negative semiconductors to achieve low power operation.

Complement – in binary logic, the opposite state.

Compilation – software process to translate source code to assembly or machine code (or error codes).

Control Flow – computer architecture involving directed flow through the program; data dependent paths are allowed.

Coprocessor – another processor to supplement the operations of the main processor. Used for floating point, video, etc. Usually relies on the main processor for instruction fetch; and control.

Cots – commercial, off-the-shelf.

CPU – central processing unit.

CSI – Camera serial interface

Dataflow – computer architecture where a changing value forces recalculation of dependent values.

DDR – dual data rate (memory).

Deadlock – a situation in which two or more competing actions are each waiting for the other to finish, and thus neither ever does.

Denorm – in floating point representation, a non-zero number with a magnitude less than the smallest normal number.

Device driver – specific software to interface a peripheral to the operating system.

Digital – using discrete values for representation of states or numbers.

Dirty bit – used to signal that the contents of a cache have changed.

DMA - direct memory access (to/from memory, for I/O devices).

Double word – two words; if word = 8 bits, double word = 16 bits.

Dram – dynamic random access memory.

EIA – Electronics Industry Association.

Epitaxial – in semiconductors, have a crystalline overlayer with a well-defined orientation.

Eprom – erasable programmable read-only memory.

EEprom – electrically erasable read-only memory.

Exception – interrupt due to internal events, such as overflow.

FET – field effect transistor.

Fetch/execute cycle – basic operating cycle of a computer; fetch the instruction, execute the instruction.

Firmware – code contained in a non-volatile memory.

Fixed point – computer numeric format with a fixed number of digits or bits, and a fixed radix point. Integers.

Flag – a binary indicator.

Flash memory – a type of non-volatile memory, similar to EEprom.

Flip-flop – a circuit with two stable states; ideal for binary.

Floating point – computer numeric format for real numbers; has significant digits and an exponent.

FPGA – field programmable gate array.

FPU – floating point unit, an ALU for floating point numbers.

Full duplex – communication in both directions simultaneously.

Gate – a circuit to implement a logic function; can have multiple inputs, but a single output.

Giga - 10^9 or 2^{30}

gpio – general purpose input, output

GPU – graphics processing unit. ALU for graphics data.

GUI – graphics user interface.

Handshake – co-ordination mechanism.

Harvard architecture – memory storage scheme with separate instructions and data.

Hexadecimal – base 16 number representation.

Hexadecimal point – radix point that separates integer from fractional values of hexadecimal numbers.

IDE – Integrated development environment for software.

IEEE – Institute of Electrical and Electronic Engineers. Professional organization and standards body.

IEEE-754 – standard for floating point representation and operations.

Infinity - the largest number that can be represented in the number system.

Integer – the natural numbers, zero, and the negatives of the natural numbers.

Interrupt – an asynchronous event to signal a need for attention (example: the phone rings).

Interrupt vector – entry in a table pointing to an interrupt service routine; indexed by interrupt number.

I/O – Input-output from the computer to external devices, or a user interface.

IoT – Internet of Things

IP – intellectual property

ISA – instruction set architecture, the software description of the computer.

ISO – International Standards Organization.

ISR – interrupt service routine, a subroutine that handles a particular interrupt event.

JTAG – Joint Test Action Group; industry group that lead to IEEE 1149.1, Standard Test Access Port and Boundary-Scan Architecture.

Junction – in semiconductors, the boundary interface of the n-type and p-type material.

Kernel – main portion of the operating system. Interface between the applications and the hardware.

Kilo – a prefix for 10^3 or 2^{10}

LAN – local area network.

Latency – time delay.

List – a data structure.

Little-endian – data format with the least significant bit or byte at the highest address, or transmitted last.

Logic operation – generally, negate, AND, OR, XOR, and their inverses.

Loop-unrolling – optimization of a loop for speed at the cost of space.

LRU – least recently used; an algorithm for item replacement in a cache.

LSB – least significant bit or byte.

LUT – look up table.

Machine language – native code for a particular computer hardware.

Mainframe – a computer you can't lift.

Mantissa – significant digits (as opposed to the exponent) of a floating point value.

Master-slave – control process with one element in charge. Master status may be exchanged among elements.

Math operation – generally, add, subtract, multiply, divide.

Mega - 10^6 or 2^{20}

Memory leak – when a program uses memory resources but does not return them, leading to a lack of available memory.

Memory scrubbing – detecting and correcting bit errors.

MESI – modified, exclusive, shared, invalid state of a cache coherency protocol.

Metaprogramming – programs that produce or modify other programs.

Microcode – hardware level data structures to translate machine instructions into sequences of circuit level operations.

Microcontroller – microprocessor with included memory and/or I/O.

Microprocessor – a monolithic cpu on a chip.

Microprogramming – modifying the microcode.

MIMD – multiple instruction, multiple data

Minicomputer – smaller than a mainframe, larger than a pc.

MIPI – Mobile Industry Processor Interface

MIPS – millions of instructions per second; sometimes used as a measure of throughput.

MMU – memory management unit; translates virtual to physical addresses.

MRAM – Magnetorestrictive random access memory. Non-volatile memory approach using magnetic storage elements and integrated circuit fabrication techniques.

MSB – most significant bit or byte.

Multiplex – combining signals on a communication channel by sampling.

Mutex – a data structure and methodology for mutual exclusion.

Multicore – multiple processing cores on one substrate or chip; need not be identical.

NAN – not-a-number; invalid bit pattern.

NAND – negated (or inverse) AND function.

NDA – non-disclosure agreement; legal agreement protecting IP.

Nibble – 4 bits, ½ byte.

NIST – National Institute of Standards and Technology (US), previously, National Bureau of Standards.

NMI – non-maskable interrupt; cannot be ignored by the software.

NMOS – negative metal oxide ssemiconductor

NOR – negated (or inverse) OR function

Normalized number – in the proper format for floating point representation.

NUMA – non-uniform memory access for multiprocessors; local and global memory access protocol.

NVM – non-volatile memory.

Octal – base 8 number.

Off-the-shelf – commercially available; not custom.

Opcode – part of a machine language instruction that specifies the operation to be performed.

Open source – methodology for hardware or software development with free distribution and access.

Operating system – software that controls the allocation of resources in a computer.

OSI – Open systems interconnect model for networking, from ISO.

Overflow - the result of an arithmetic operation exceeds the capacity of the destination.

Paging – memory management technique using fixed size memory blocks.

Paradigm – a pattern or model

Paradigm shift – a change from one paradigm to another. Disruptive or evolutionary.

Parallel – multiple operations or communication proceeding simultaneously.

Parity – an error detecting mechanism involving an extra check bit in the word.

PC – personal computer, politically correct, program counter.

PCB – printed circuit board.

PCI – peripheral interconnect interface (bus).

Peta - 10^{15} or 2^{50}

Pinout – mapping of signals to I/O pins of a device.

Pipeline – operations in serial, assembly-line fashion.

Pixel – picture element; smallest addressable element on a display or a sensor..

PROM – programmable read-only memory.

Quad word – four words. If word = 16 bits, quad word is 64 bits.

Queue – first in, first out data buffer structure; hardware of software.

Radix point – separates integer and fractional parts of a real number.

RAM – random access memory; any item can be access in the same time as any other.

RAS – Row address strobe, in dram refresh.

Register – temporary storage location for a data item.

Reset – signal and process that returns the hardware to a known, defined state.

RISC – reduced instruction set computer.

ROM – read only memory.

Real-time – system that responds to events in a predictable, bounded time..

Sandbox – an isolated and controlled environment to run untested or potentially malicious code.

SDRAM – synchronous dynamic random access memory.

Segmentation – dividing a network or memory into sections.

Self-modifying code – computer code that modifies itself as it run; hard to debug

Semiconductor – material with electrical characteristics between conductors and insulators; basis of current technology processor and memory devices.

Semaphore –signaling element among processes.

Serial – bit by bit.

Server – a computer running services on a network.

Shift – move one bit position to the left or right in a word.

Sign-magnitude – number representation with a specific sign bit.

Signed number – representation with a value and a numeric sign.

SIMD – single instruction, multiple data.

SIMM – single in-line memory module.

SOC – system on chip

Software – set of instructions and data to tell a computer what to do.

SMP – symmetric multiprocessing.

SRAM – static random access memory.

SSE – Streaming SIMD Extensions

Stack – first in, last out data structure. Can be hardware of software.

Stack pointer – a reference pointer to the top of the stack.

State machine – model of sequential processes.

Superscalar – computer with instruction-level parallelism, by replication of resources.

Synchronous – using the same clock to coordinate operations.

System – a collection of interacting elements and relationships with a specific behavior.

Table – data structure. Can be multi-dimensional.

Tera - 10^{12} or 2^{40}

Test-and-set – coordination mechanism for multiple processes that allows reading to a location and writing it in a non-interruptible manner.

Thread – smallest independent set of instructions managed by a multiprocessing operating system.

TLB – translation lookaside buffer – a cache of addresses.

TRAP – exception or fault handling mechanism in a computer; an operating system component.

Triplicate – using three copies (of hardware, software, messaging, power supplies, etc.). for redundancy and error control.

Truncate – discard. Cutoff, make shorter.

TSX – transactional sync extensions

TTL – transistor-transistor logic in digital integrated circuits. (1963).

UART – universal asynchronous receiver transmitter.

Underflow – the result of an arithmetic operation is smaller than the smallest representable number.

Unsigned number – a number without a numeric sign.

USB – universal serial bus

Vector – single dimensional array of values.

VHDL- very high level description language; a language to describe integrated circuits and asic/ fpga's.

VIA – vertical conducting pathway through an insulating layer in a semiconductor.

Virtual memory – memory management technique using address translation.

Virtualization – creating a virtual resource from available physical resources.

Virus – malignant computer program.

VLIW – very long instruction word – mechanism for parallelism.

von Neumann – John, a computer pioneer and mathematician; realized that computer instructions are data.

Wiki – the Hawaiian word for "quick." Refers to a collaborative content website.

Word – a collection of bits of any size; does not have to be a power of two.

Write-back – cache organization where the data is not written to main memory until the cache location is needed for re-use.

Write-through – all cache writes also go to memory.

X86 – Intel -16, -32, 64-bit ISA.

XOR – exclusive OR; either but not both

Bibliography

Agarwal, Rakesh K. *80X86 Architecture and Programming: Architecture Reference : Covers Implementations from the 8086 to the I486, and Includes the 80X87 Processor,* Prentice Hall (January 1991), ISBN-10: 0132454327.

Antonakos, James L. *Introduction to the Intel Family of Microprocessors: A Hands-On Approach Utilizing the 80x86 Microprocessor Family* (3rd Edition), Prentice Hall; 3rd edition (June 3, 1998), ISBN-10: 0138934398.

Brey, Barry B. *Intel 32-Bit Microprocessor: 80386, 80486, and Pentium* Prentice Hall; 1 edition (September 16, 1994), ISBN-10: 002314260X.

Brey, Barry B. *Intel Microprocessors 8086/8088, 80186, 80286, 80386, 80486, The: Architecture, Programming, and Interfacing,* Prentice Hall; 4 edition (November 18, 1996), ISBN-10: 0132606704.

Brey, Barry B. *Advanced Intel Microprocessors: 80286, 80386, And 80486,* Merrill Pub Co (August 1992), ISBN-10: 0023142456.

Brumm, Penn; Brumm, Don; Scanlon, Leo J. *80486 Programming,* Windcrest, 1991, ISBN 0-8306-7577-9.

Das, Lyla B. *The x86 Microprocessors: 8086 to Pentium, Multicores, Atom and the 8051 Microcontroller, 2/e: Programming and Interfacing,* 2014, ASIN- B00Q8L2IKU.

Detmer, Richard C. *Introduction to 80X86 Assembly Language and Computer Architecture* Jones & Bartlett Pub; (February 2001), ISBN-10: 0763717738.

Edelhart, Michael *Intel's Official Guide to 386 Computing,* McGraw-Hill Osborne Media (March 1991), ISBN-10: 0078816939.

Intel, *80286 and 80287 Programmer's Reference Manual*, Intel, 1987, 210498.

Intel, *80286 Hardware Reference Manual*, Intel, 210760.

Intel, *80286 Operating Systems Writer's Guide*, 121960.

Intel, 80387 Programmer's Reference Manual, 1987 ISBN 1-55512-057-1.

Intel, 80386 System Software Writer's Guide, 1987, 231499.

Intel i486 Microprocessor, 1989, 240440-001.

Intel, *80386 Programmer's Reference Manual*, Intel, 1987, ISBN 1-55512-057-1.

Irvine, Kip R. *Assembly Language for x86 Processors* Prentice Hall; 6 edition (March 7, 2010), ISBN-10: 013602212X.

Leinecker, Richard C. "Processor-Detection Schemes," Dr. Dobb's Journal, 1993 v 18 i 6 p 46.

Morse, Stephan and Albert, Douglas *The 80286 Architecture*, Wiley Books, 1986, ISBN 0 471-83185-9.

Myers, Ben "Some Assembly Still Required," PC Tech Journal, 03/01/89.

Rash, Bill "iAPX 286 Loadall Instruction," Intel Technical Memo, November 21, 1984.

Ruth, Ed *Building Coffee Lake a Guide to Building a Powerful Personal Computer: Intel Core i7-8700K and socket LGA-1151 using a Z370 Gigabyte Gaming Motherboard with 32GB of DDR4 RAM,* 2018, ASIN-B07BLSJ44V.

Scanlon, Leo, *8086/8088 Assembly Language Programming*, Brady Books, 1984, ISBN 0-89303-424-X.

Scanlon, Leo J. *8086/8088/80286 Assembly Language*, (Revised Edition), Brady Books,1988, ISBN 0-13-246919-7.

Shanley, Tom *Protected Mode Software Architecture,* Addison-Wesley Professional; 1 edition (March 16, 1996), ISBN-10: 020155447X.

Shanley, Tom *80486 System Architecture* (3rd Edition), Addison Wesley Longman; 3rd Sub edition, January 1995, ISBN-10: 0201409941.

Skinner, Thomas *An Introduction to Assembly Language Programming for the 8086 Family*, Wiley, 1985, $18.95,ISBN0-471-80825-3.

Stakem, Patrick H. *Floating Point Computation*, 2013, PRRB Publishing, ASIN-B00D5E1S7W.

Strauss, Edmund *80386 Technical Reference*, Brady Books, 1987, ISBN 0-13-246893-X.

Theis, Klaus-Dieter *The Innovative 80X86 Architectures: The 80286 Microprocessor,* Prentice Hall (January 1991), ISBN-10: 0134672836.

Triebel, Walter A. *The 80386, 80486, and Pentium Microprocessor: Hardware, Software, and Interfacing,* Prentice Hall; 1 edition (October 3, 1997), ISBN-10: 0135332257.

Uffenbeck, John T*he 80x86 Family: Design, Programming, and Interfacing* (3rd Edition) Prentice Hall; 3 edition (February 14, 2001), ISBN-10: 0130257117.

wikipedia, various.

Willen, David and Krantz, Jeffrey *8088 Assembler Language Programming: The IBM PC* (2nd ed), Sams, 1983, ISBN0-672-22400-3.

Wilt, Nicholas "Assembly Language Programming for the 80x87," Dr. Dobb's Journal 1992 v 17 i 3 P. 36.

MicroDesign Resources ,*The Complete x86: The Definitive Guide to 386, 486, and the Pentium-class Microprocessors*, (1994), ISBN-10: 1885330022.

Understanding X86 Microprocessors: 99 Articles Originally Published in Microprocessor Report Between September 1987 and April 1993 Ziff Davis Press, June 1993), ISBN-10: 1562761587

If you enjoyed this book, you might also enjoy one of my other books in the Computer Architecture series. Most are also available in printed edition as well.

Stakem, Patrick H. *16-bit Microprocessors, History and Architecture*, 2013 PRRB Publishing, ASIN-B00D5ETQ3U.

Stakem, Patrick H. *4- and 8-bit Microprocessors, Architecture and History*, 2013, PRRB Publishing, ASIN-B00D5ZSKCC.

Stakem, Patrick H. *Apollo's Computers*, 2014, PRRB Publishing, ASIN B00LDT217.

Stakem, Patrick H. *The Architecture and Applications of the ARM Microprocessors*, 2013, PRRB Publishing, ASIN-B00BAFF4OQ.

Stakem, Patrick H. *Embedded Computer Systems, Volume 1, Introduction and Architecture*, 2013, PRRB Publishing, ASIN-00GB0W4GG.

Stakem, Patrick H. *The History of Spacecraft Computers from the V-2 to the Space Station*, 2013, PRRB Publishing, ASIN-B004L626U6.

Stakem, Patrick H. *Floating Point Computation*, 2013, PRRB Publishing, ASIN-B00D5E1S7W.

Stakem, Patrick H. *Architecture of Massively Parallel Microprocessor Systems*, 2011, PRRB Publishing, ASIN-B004K1F172.

Stakem, Patrick H. *Multicore Computer Architecture,* 2014, PRRB Publishing, ASIN B00KB2XIQD.

Stakem, Patrick H. *Personal Robots*, 2014, PRRB Publishing, ASIN-BOOMBQ084K.

Stakem, Patrick H. *RISC Microprocessors, History and Overview*, 2013, PRRB Publishing, ASIN B00D5SCHQO.

Stakem, Patrick H. *Robots and Telerobots in Space Applications*, 2011, PRRB Publishing, ASIN-B0057IMJRM.
.
Stakem, Patrick H. Microprocessors in Space, 2011, PRRB Publishing, ASIN-B0057PFJQI.

Stakem, Patrick H. *Computer Virtualization and the Cloud*, 2013, PRRB Publishing, ASIN-B00BAFF0JA.

Stakem, Patrick H. *What's the Worst That Could Happen? Bad Assumptions, Ignorance, Failures and Screw-ups in Engineering Projects*, 2014, PRRB Publishing, ASIN-B00JSH540.

Stakem, Patrick H. *Computer Architecture & Programming of the Intel x86 Family*, 2013, PRRB Publishing, ASIN-B008Q39D4.

Stakem, Patrick H. *The Hardware and Software Architecture of the Transputer*, 2011, PRRB Publishing, ASIN B004OYTS1K.

Stakem, Patrick H. *Mainframes, Computing on Big Iron*, 2015, PRRB Publishing, ASIN-B00TXQQ3FI.

Stakem, Patrick H. *Embedded in Space*, 2015, PRRB Publishing, ASIN-B018BAYCCM.

Stakem, Patrick H. *Extreme Environment Embedded Systems*, PRRB Publishing, ASIN-B01AF9CBM0, Jan, 2016.

Stakem, Patrick H. *Introduction to Spacecraft Control Centers*, 2015, PRRB Publishing, ASIN-B01D1Y5LZ0.

Stakem, Patrick H. *Graphics Processing Units, an overview*, 2017, PRRB Publishing, ASIN-B06XJB4VFV.

Stakem, Patrick H. *Intel Embedded and the Arduino-101*, 2017, PRRB Publishing, ASIN-B06XJR1739.